3-30-99

To Rick,
fellow leader at ARINC
Best wishes for every future success!
Ray Wenderlich

THE ABCs OF SUCCESSFUL LEADERSHIP

Proven, Practical Attitudes, Behaviors & Concepts Based on Core Values that Result in Successful Leadership

Raymond L. Wenderlich

First Edition

Success Builders, Inc.
Ellicott City, Maryland

The ABCs of Successful Leadership
Proven, Practical Attitudes, Behaviors & Concepts Based on Core Values that Result in Successful Leadership
By Raymond L. Wenderlich

Published by:
Success Builders, Inc.
Post Office Box 1686
Ellicott City, MD 21041

Copyright © 1997 by Raymond L. Wenderlich
First Printing 1997
Printed in the United States of America

Publisher's Cataloging-in-Publication
(Prepared by Quality Books Inc.)

Wenderlich, Raymond L.
    The ABCs of successful leadership : proven, practical, attitudes, behaviors & concepts based on core values that result in successful leadership / Raymond L. Wenderlich. -- 1st ed.
    p. cm.
    Preassigned LCCN: 97-67753
    ISBN 0-9658831-2-4

    1. Leadership.   2. Employee motivation.   I. Title

HD57.7.W46 1997   658.4'092
                                         QB197-40843

DEDICATION

*To the multitude of
leaders and followers who
have helped me throughout the years.*

USE OF THIS BOOK

It is my hope that this book will not be read once and put away on a bookshelf. It needs to be read, re-read, reviewed in small chunks, pondered over, and discussed.

Most importantly, it needs to be translated into specific actions.

Readers are encouraged to take written notes and to record specific actions they intend to take. Thus, the book can become a valuable personal reference and blueprint for each person's leadership journey.

Perhaps the most effective use of this book is in a seminar or workshop situation, where the group leader facilitates a discussion of each of the concepts in the book, and draws upon the wisdom and experience of the group. For, while no individual knows everything about good leadership, my experience indicates that most groups of leaders collectively know most of the key leadership principles.

It is my hope that you will use the concepts presented in this book, add more of your own, and thereby grow and prosper as a leader.

— RLW

TABLE OF CONTENTS

INTRODUCTION

This book began as my answer to a question raised by my son and by people with whom I work. The question was, "What makes you an effective and respected leader?"

As I pondered this question, I realized that although the answer is not simple, it is also not rocket science. I have found that there are a finite number of attitudes, behaviors, and concepts based on core values that I have seen result in successful leadership. These attitudes, behaviors, and concepts can be applied by anyone in any type of leadership position.

During my 24 years of successful leadership experience, I have accumulated some very valuable leadership ideas that are practical, field-tested in a number of different disciplines, and proven to succeed consistently.

These ideas are based on solid values, and are the opposite of the results-at-all-costs theories espoused by some. While the results-at-all-costs approach can achieve goals and objectives, this approach often leaves people feeling bitter, disrespected and, for the long term, demotivated. The leadership approach and ideas that I offer in this book are timeless and are oriented toward long-term success with proper regard for the people being led. By consistent application of sound principles based on morally sound values, I have built teams and led people to be successful in a number of diverse arenas.

I recognize that most leaders don't have time to read 300-page books and extract the key leadership principles scattered throughout them. They need something more focused and easier to read. What makes this book valuable and unique is that it has captured a considerable number of proven, practical ideas in a simple, straightforward, digestible format.

This book is for people who want to achieve personal success by getting superior results from the organizations they lead. Effective leadership is the key to achieving superior results. I've provided a number of practical, proven attitudes, behaviors, and concepts that will help you to achieve the personal success you desire.

Carefully consider each idea in this book. Continuously challenge and improve yourself as a leader and thereby, achieve better results through the people you lead.

I wish you every success.

— RLW

CHAPTER 1

The Top Ten Principles of Successful Leadership

It is my experience, that there is a large but finite number of factors that contribute to successful leadership. I have studied many leaders and have picked out what has worked for me and what I have seen work for them. To help you to get started and to focus, I've listed in this chapter what I consider to be the top ten principles (attitudes, behaviors, and concepts) that most significantly contribute to effective leadership. If you can internalize and implement these ten principles, I believe that you will be able to significantly increase your success as a leader.

1

A Learning Attitude

Decide, right now, to be a lifelong student of leadership.

Learn from every leader you encounter —

by what they do that's effective,

by what they do that's ineffective, and

by what they fail to do.

An Overall Strategy

Attract, select, and retain excellent people.

Make certain your people fully understand your expectations.

Give your people everything they need to do their jobs: direction, leadership, information, tools, management support, training, and appropriate resources.

Empower them and hold them accountable, then get out of their way and "watch their smoke." There's no need to oversupervise them.

Caring About Your People

Treat your people as your most prized resource — because they are.

Act as though your very job depends on how you treat your people — because it does.

Outstanding leaders care deeply about their people.

Leaders vs. Managers

Always think of yourself primarily as a leader — not as a manager or a supervisor.

Inventories, materials, and problems can be managed.

People can't be managed — they must be led.

Vision

A large part of your job as a leader is to create a clear, compelling vision for your team.

This is crucial for success and cannot be delegated.

A compelling vision is one of the most powerful forces on earth.

Integrity

Your integrity is among your most valuable possessions. It must never be compromised.

Your people's integrity is among their most valuable possessions.

Hold your people to your same high standards for integrity. The vast majority of them will respond to your leadership.

Inverted Pyramid Organization Concept

Use the inverted pyramid organization concept. The customer is the boss. Within your organization, the people who directly serve the customer are the bosses.

Ensure that your organization fully supports the people who directly serve the customer.

Focus

Use the 80-20 rule (Pareto Principle).

Twenty percent of your activities yield eighty percent of the results.

FOCUS-FOCUS-FOCUS on the few areas that will make or break you and your team.

If you want to be an effective leader, you can't allow yourself the luxury of trying to attend to everything equally.

Concentrate

Concentrate on people (including customers), safety, quality, and goals.

Most of the rest will take care of itself.

Knowing Your Objectives

Be very serious about your two main objectives:
- the team winning the ballgame, and
- your players being all they can be

But be sure to have a lot of fun pursuing these objectives.

NOTES

What key elements do you want to focus on from this section of the book?

_____

_____

_____

_____

_____

_____

_____

_____

_____

_____

What specific actions will you take?

_____

_____

_____

_____

_____

_____

_____

_____

_____

_____

Additional
Attitudes,
Behaviors &
Concepts
Based on Core Values

The next eight chapters are a collection of additional leadership principles, based on core values, that I've learned in my career. They really do work!

I understand that results can be achieved using the results-at-all-costs approach and sometimes this approach is very efficient timewise. However, this short-term approach may not build teams, boost morale or be respected by followers, peers or other leaders.

Leadership based on core values such as integrity, discipline, loyalty, responsibility, and courage results in a followership that wants to be led and feels good about what they are doing.

Additionally, organizations will take on the characteristics of their leaders. In an organization based on core values, there is nothing to hide, nothing to be ashamed of. As a result, efforts can be focused on the work at hand and not cover-ups, politics, or back peddling. Ultimately, the leadership and organizations that are fundamentally based on core values, will be more effective and efficient than leadership and organizations that subscribe to less effective approaches.

CHAPTER 2
Integrity

You are the ex officio moral and ethical leader of your organization. Recognize this and take this responsibility very seriously. Nobody else can provide proper moral and ethical leadership for your team.

"In matters of style, swim with the current; in matters of principle, stand like a rock."

— Thomas Jefferson

Strong leaders combine strategy and character to achieve success. Of these, only strategy is expendable.

Never violate a confidence. People must know that they can talk with you privately without any fear that you will ever misuse the information. You will certainly be tempted to violate this rule. Make a decision *now* that you will keep the confidences of those with whom you interact.

"The supreme quality for a leader is unquestionably integrity."

— Dwight D. Eisenhower

Boldly do what you believe is right. Don't be overly concerned with what people think about it. People are not the One you need to impress.

"When principle is involved, be deaf to expediency."
— Commodore Maury, 1849

"To thine own self be true and as night follows day thou cannot be false to any man."

— William Shakespeare

NOTES

What key elements do you want to focus on from this section of the book?

_____

_____

_____

_____

_____

_____

_____

_____

_____

_____

_____

What specific actions will you take?

_____

_____

_____

_____

_____

_____

_____

_____

_____

_____

_____

CHAPTER 3
Discipline &
Continuous Improvement

Write and "approve" your own personal mission statement, clearly stating what you consider to be your mission in life. Then refer to this mission statement frequently. If you can lead yourself successfully, perhaps you can lead others.

Develop an excellent self-assessment program for your operation. Require of yourself and of your team the ability to find and correct your own problems. All outstanding teams have outstanding self-assessment capability.

When someone criticizes the performance or methods of your group, thank them for speaking up, and listen carefully to what they have to say. More often than not, their comments will lead you to a flawed process. Such occasions are no time for defensiveness. They are great opportunities to improve your operation.

Set tough but achievable goals for your operation. Write them down. Review them with your people frequently. If you have written goals, you have a chance to achieve them.

Exhibit a questioning attitude. Maintain a healthy dissatisfaction with the status-quo. Ask the not-so-dumb questions:

- Why are we doing it this way?

- Can we change it to be simpler or more logical?

- Can we minimize handoffs?

Continuous improvement is crucial to your success and even your survival.

Continually display a sense of urgency about your work and about improving the way you do business (as opposed to going-with-the-flow, or business-as-usual attitudes).

When you're agonizing over how to handle a difficult personnel situation, ask yourself how you'd handle it if the employee were your son, daughter, nephew, niece, aunt or uncle. If you answer yourself honestly, you'll have your answer on how to handle the situation.

"You do not lead by hitting people over the head — that's assault, not leadership."

— Dwight D. Eisenhower

NOTES

What key elements do you want to focus on from this section of the book?

_____

_____

_____

_____

_____

_____

_____

_____

_____

_____

_____

What specific actions will you take?

_____

_____

_____

_____

_____

_____

_____

_____

_____

_____

CHAPTER 4
Caring About Your People & Customers

Always remember — you need your people more than they need you.

Empathic listening is an important skill of a good leader. It involves paraphrasing back to the speaker your understanding of their most significant ideas, opinions, and feelings.

Become skilled at empathic listening, which assures that you understand the other person and, more importantly, that they *feel* understood (do this before you share your awesome wisdom with them).

Billions of people on this earth go to bed hungry for an honest word of appreciation.

Don't contribute to this problem!

Don't be too reluctant to create a significant emotional event (e.g., a change-or-you'll-be-fired discussion) for one of your employees. Sometimes it's exactly what they need to make a big change in their behavior or habits.

Empower your workers to care about and act on their customers' needs first.

Set aside some time on a regular basis for "fireside chats." Simply schedule a place and time where you will be available to chat about whatever your people want to talk about. No agendas. No fancy speeches. Just plain talk.

Work hard at establishing close ties with your teammates at the worker level. Consider this:

As a leader, you have the power to fix problems and effect significant change but you frequently lack detailed knowledge of *what* to fix and change and *how* to fix and change it.

Your worker-level people on the other hand have detailed knowledge of *what* to fix and change and *how* to fix and change it. Yet they often lack sufficient power to fix the problems and effect significant change.

If you can establish close ties with your people at the worker level, you can effectively bring to bear the power to make changes and improvements in the areas where they are most needed.

When disciplining employees, use the minimum amount of discipline necessary to get their attention. Administering too much discipline will not gain you respect for being "tough," and might seriously damage the spirit and loyalty of your employees.

"Encourage (indeed, cherish) diversity of opinion, of experience, of style, of approach on your team. Welcome and embrace the dynamics of differences that come from age, gender, race and other artificial dividers of our cultures."

— Charles E. (Chuck) Faughnan

Treat your people as customers, because they are the principal customers of your personal leadership services. Similarly, if you want to know who the best leaders are in your organization, simply ask your people.

It's just like asking students in school whom the best teachers are. You don't need the principal to sit in on classes — the students already know! Like the students, your people are the best judges of the quality of the services (leadership) that they receive.

For crucial tasks that your people are required to perform, you need to have a process whereby you verify that they can perform the task. Don't make the mistake of merely giving them the information they need to perform the task and assuming they will be able to successfully assimilate the information. Make sure they can do it; don't set them up for failure.

When making personnel-selection decisions within your organization, choose the optimal combination of ability and availability (how available the person is for the assignment). Sometimes (especially for promotions), ability is of paramount importance. In other circumstances, ability and availability are of equal importance. Occasionally, for less-involved, short-term tasks, availability of the person is the main consideration. Give some thought to the proper combination for the given circumstance.

For promotions, when considering an employee's ability, be sure to include consideration of their ability to handle increased responsibility in the future (their long-term potential).

Spend a lot of time developing your people. You won't be given 100 percent all-stars on your team. Your job is to develop your ordinary people into all-stars.

"Catch people doing something right!"

— Ken Blanchard

Lurking around to catch people doing something wrong is not leadership, it's spying.

Spend a lot of time with your people. Put it on your calendar.

Corollary: Don't be a desk potato. Be sure to spend significant time wandering around and talking to your people. Help them to feel free to talk with you about things that are on their minds. It's not enough merely to have an open-door policy.

Spend a lot of time with your customers. Put it on your calendar.

Corollary: Frequently ask them for feedback on your group's performance. Welcome their complaints. Don't assume your group is performing as wonderfully for the customer as your people tell you it is.

Pay a lot of attention to hiring. Getting the right people is at least half the battle. Hiring is one of your most important responsibilities.

More on hiring: Never hire people based on what they say they will do for you; hire based on what they have done (because they'll probably continue to do it). For example, a .250 lifetime hitter will probably continue to hit .250 after he changes teams.

NOTES

What key elements do you want to focus on from this section of the book?

_____

_____

_____

_____

_____

_____

_____

_____

_____

What specific actions will you take?

_____

_____

_____

_____

_____

_____

_____

_____

_____

CHAPTER 5
Accountability, Responsibility & Goal Setting

There is no substitute for personal accountability. For important tasks and duties, make certain there is a person who is personally accountable for the results — good or bad. However, insist that you be held ultimately accountable for the results of your group.

"Never reward activity. Always reward results. But always monitor activity and behavior as they pertain to results."

— Jim Hackett
President, Bunker Hill
Consulting Group

Expect, with rare exceptions, that assignments and commitments get done on time. It saves embarrassment and time! Conversely, if you routinely allow assignments and commitments to be completed late, then people have the additional task of explaining to someone why they're late.

This is not to say you shouldn't renegotiate due-dates to ensure that you and your people are working on the most *important* tasks vs. the most *urgent* tasks.

On autonomy and accountability:

Either tell your people how to do their job but don't hold them accountable for results,

or

Hold them totally accountable for results and let them do their job pretty much their own way.

It's not fair to tell them exactly how to do their job and then hold them accountable for the results.

Define your requirements.

When you ask for something from someone, always include a date you'd like to receive it. You'll almost always get it faster with a due date, than if you leave it open-ended.

"Don't confuse activity with accomplishment!"

— unknown

For your team, be sure to develop a comprehensive set of performance indicators. These indicators should collectively tell a complete story of how successfully your team is performing. Give much personal attention to the establishment and measurement of these performance indicators. They are a key to success.

Display these measurements for all the team to see. Expect each team member to show individual contributions in support of these performance indicators.

You will get most of what you measure. You will get even more of what you pay for (reward). So be really careful of what you measure and what you reward.

If someone, after reasonable effort on your part, can't or won't deliver what you need:

Don't ignore it. If you do, you've taught them that it's acceptable to ignore you.

Don't have your boss call them. If you do, you've taught them that it's acceptable to ignore you. They've learned that if it's really important, your boss will call.

Do get your boss to talk to their boss. If you do this, you've taught them that if they ignore you, they'll hear from their boss.

(If you both report to the same person, work it out or constructively escalate the issue to your mutual boss.)

Require a strong results-orientation of yourself and your team. Process is nice, but don't get overly enamored with process at the expense of results. The outcome is what counts. Keep your eye on the bottom line.

Don't get overly excited about how much progress you've made. Keep focused on the difference between where you are and where you need to be (your team's present status vs. what your team needs to achieve).

NOTES

What key elements do you want to focus on from this section of the book?

_____

_____

_____

_____

_____

_____

_____

_____

_____

_____

_____

What specific actions will you take?

_____

_____

_____

_____

_____

_____

_____

_____

_____

_____

_____

CHAPTER 6
Loyalty

Be loyal to your bosses, helpful to your peers, and generous to your subordinates.

"Trust is the emotional glue that binds followers and leaders together."

— Warren Bennis and Burt Nanus

Source: *Leaders* (second edition, 1997)
HarperCollins Publishers

You must always be true to your people and worthy of their trust.

"Be true to your school."

Demonstrate complete loyalty to your boss and to your organization. Be a positive representative of your team and your organization. If you can't do this, change jobs. Don't degrade *yourself* by exhibiting disloyalty.

Make loyalty one of your towering strengths.

Loyalty does not require blind obedience.

It's OK and encouraged to disagree with your boss in private, but when a decision is made and you walk out that door, you must project full support, commitment, and ownership for the decision.

(Exceptions to this rule include illegal, immoral, and unethical decisions.)

Loyalty in organizations is important on at least three planes. You must be loyal to your leader, to your team, and to yourself. Normally, you can feel and act loyal on all three planes. However, you may occasionally find yourself in a situation where loyalty to all three is impossible. In these situations, think things through carefully — the answers are not always obvious.

Dealing with disloyalty:

If you suspect one of your people is displaying disloyal behavior, you must act quickly and decisively. It's a great opportunity to be very clear to this person about your standards for loyalty and the consequences of disloyalty. This is not the time to waver, to delay or to hope it goes away by itself.

NOTES

What key elements do you want to focus on from this section of the book?

_____

_____

_____

_____

_____

_____

_____

_____

_____

_____

What specific actions will you take?

_____

_____

_____

_____

_____

_____

_____

_____

_____

_____

CHAPTER 7
Courage & Perseverance

"Nothing will ever be attempted if all possible objections must be first overcome."

— unknown

Develop in yourself and in your organization a strong bias for action. Many situations call for the *ready-fire-aim* approach. Don't analyze things to death. Don't be a victim of *paralysis by analysis*. Make decisions and encourage your people to do the same.

"Don't be afraid to go out on the limb. That's where the fruit is."

— unknown

"Nothing in the world can take the place of persistence. Talent will not; nothing is more common than unsuccessful men with great talent. Genius will not; unrewarded genius is almost a proverb. Education will not; the world is full of educated derelicts. Persistence and determination alone are omnipotent."

— Calvin Coolidge

If you see a sign that says, "Don't bring me problems — bring me solutions," take it down and throw it into the trash can. Encourage your people to speak up and tell you about problems *even if they don't have solutions or a recommendation*. If you don't hear about the problems, rest assured (1) the problems still exist and (2) your customers, your competitors, and your bosses *will* hear about them.

"Obstacles are those frightful things you see when you take your eyes off your goals."

— unknown

Reasonable people adapt themselves to the conditions that surround them. All progress depends on us unreasonable people.

If you really want to be respected as a leader, you must be able to stand alone when the going gets tough. Your people have to know that you will do the right thing in the face of adversity — even if it hurts you personally to do so. People will follow such a leader *anywhere*.

"Do not follow where the path may lead. Go instead where there is no path and leave a trail."

— unknown

It is better to be boldly decisive and risk a mistake than to overanalyze and miss the window of opportunity.

NOTES

What key elements do you want to focus on from this section of the book?

_____

_____

_____

_____

_____

_____

_____

_____

_____

_____

What specific actions will you take?

_____

_____

_____

_____

_____

_____

_____

_____

_____

_____

CHAPTER 8
Being Positive

Success in life and in leadership is 85 percent attitude and 15 percent aptitude. So spend a lot of effort causing yourself to think, act, and speak positively. Avoid negativism (some people call it "being practical") in yourself and others.

"There's no limit to what you can achieve if you don't mind who gets the credit."

— unknown

"Be a cheerleader for your team and organization. Take time to celebrate successes and share the positive results with your people."

— Charles E. (Chuck) Faughnan

"We are continually faced with great opportunities, brilliantly disguised as insolvable problems."

— unknown

Be very proficient at feedback, especially *positive* feedback. You should aim for a 10:1 ratio between the positive and negative feedback you provide to your people.

Praise in public. Criticize in private.

Praise the person and their performance; criticize the performance, not the person.

This is timeless advice that works! If you ever forget it, you will get into trouble immediately.

NOTES

What key elements do you want to focus on from this section of the book?

_____

_____

_____

_____

_____

_____

_____

_____

_____

_____

_____

What specific actions will you take?

_____

_____

_____

_____

_____

_____

_____

_____

_____

_____

_____

CHAPTER 9

More Ideas For
Leaders To Think About

You are an effective leader to the extent that your people respect you and will follow you.

Maintain a proper balance of concern for tasks, results, and people. Any time you get out of balance, your effectiveness and the effectiveness of your team will suffer.

Setting the proper example is perhaps the greatest tool a leader has to influence his/her followers.

So lead by *example*, not by *edict*.

"A meeting is no substitute for progress."

— unknown

So try not to derive a lot of satisfaction from the number of meetings you hold or attend.

Quality is not a department. It is an organization-wide commitment.

Great leaders help their people to reject an entitlement mentality, in favor of a pay-for-results philosophy.

True job security comes not from a policy book, but from one's personal skills and the extent to which one helps their team or organization to be competitive and successful.

When was the last time you washed a rental car?

Translation: Ownership and accountability are crucial for success.

Make good decisions about the relative importance of efficiency vs. effectiveness. In many situations, efficiency is very important. In other situations, achieving effectiveness is crucial, even if the activity is done inefficiently. Don't over-focus on efficiency.

How many standing ovations have you *led* in your lifetime?

Good leaders are good at putting people into positions that maximize their strengths and minimize their weaknesses. Many times, a person who is struggling in one job might excel in another job that is better aligned with his/her strengths.

How many morally sound, but politically incorrect or unpopular causes are you actively involved in?

You could be missing out on some prime leadership opportunities.

"There is something that is much more scarce, something rarer than ability. It is the ability to recognize ability."

— unknown

"There is nothing as useless as doing efficiently what should not be done at all."

— Peter F. Drucker

You have no obligation to handle everything that finds its way into your in-box. Be selective about what you decide to handle. Many things should be delegated to your people. Many more things should be relegated to the trash can.

Good leaders should become very skilled at conflict resolution. Don't easily accept any *win-lose* or *compromise* solutions that don't fully satisfy either party. Look for *win-win* solutions. Such solutions normally work, stand the test of time, and promote strong relationships.

There are eagles and there are ducks. You may have some eagles that are brilliantly disguised as ducks. If so, help them to find the "zipper" in their costumes so they can get out and everyone can see that they are eagles. But if you conclude that they are really ducks ... don't send them to eagle school.

In organizations, what you can accomplish as an individual is negligible compared to what you can accomplish as part of the larger team. Engender in yourself and in your people a strong sense of association with team success. Help your people to accept and nurture their interdependence on each other.

There is no such thing as failure. We sometimes encounter undesirable outcomes, which we should treat as learning experiences for our team. How we treat undesirable outcomes has everything to do with how successful our team becomes.

Good leadership is the art of getting average people to willingly do superior work.

Leadership is not the same as supervision.

Did you ever hear of a Marine platoon commander supervising his troops into battle?

Good leaders are much more scarce than good supervisors.

In most cases, the performance and success of a team is limited not by the team's resources, skills or procedures, but by the imagination and vision of its leader.

If strong leadership were a crime, would your people have enough evidence to convict you?

Go back to the beginning. Review these again. Implement them in your life. Improve on them. Good luck!

NOTES

What key elements do you want to focus on from this section of the book?

_____

_____

_____

_____

_____

_____

_____

_____

_____

What specific actions will you take?

_____

_____

_____

_____

_____

_____

_____

_____

_____

AFTERWORD

I sincerely hope you've enjoyed this book as much as I've enjoyed putting it together.

Please allow me to once again emphasize that these ideas are not theoretical exercises. They are proven concepts. Throughout my career, I have used them successfully and observed them to really work in real-life leadership situations. I hope you will give them a try and that you will commit yourself to the lifelong study of the art of successful leadership.

I pray for your success.

— RLW

ACKNOWLEDGMENTS

I thank God for my life and this "journey."

I thank my family (Vicki, Ray and Amy) for their love and support.

I thank the many people who have helped me to put this book together. The book is much better for the insightful reviews by Chuck Faughnan, Jim Hinson, Debbie Miller, Cris Packard, Courtenay Pecoraro, Brian Smith, Pat Walsh, Patty Waters, and Bob Wenderlich. Floyd Fontanilla did a super job with the cover and book design. P.K. Daniel, an editor for the Los Angeles Daily News, was a kind yet thorough line editor.

I sincerely appreciate all the help, instruction, encouragement and patience given to me over the years by a multitude of people as I've taken my long journey in the field of leadership. Thanks to Chris Poindexter, George Creel, Fr. Paul Dudziak, Bill Gautier, and many others. My leadership style is adapted from the behaviors, attitudes, and ideas of those mentioned and many other fine leaders.

I've found that over the years, many a good idea "sticks" but sometimes its source doesn't. I ask forgiveness from any source of any idea in this book whom I may have inadvertently failed to properly identify.

In particular, I wish to thank the many fine people that I've had the privilege of leading. Their support, followership and professionalism have impressed me profoundly. The leadership awards they have given me are among my most prized possessions. I will remember these people always.

— RLW

The ABCs of
SUCCESSFUL LEADERSHIP

ORDER INFORMATION

Did you borrow this book?
Do you want a copy of your own?
Do you want a great gift for a friend, relative,
co-worker or boss?
Please make a copy of this page, provide all necessary
information and send with check or money order
(made out to Success Builders, Inc.) to:

**Success Builders, Inc.
P.O. Box 1686-101
Ellicott City, MD 21041**

Name _____

Address _____
City _____

State _____ Zipcode _____

Book Total ($21.95 U.S. or $29.95 CAN. each) $_____

Shipping & handling ($2.00 for first copy and $_____
$1.00 for each additional copy)

Applicable Sales Tax (MD residents add 5%) $_____

Total Amount Due $_____

Success Builders books are available at special quantity discounts for bulk purchases for sales promotions, premiums, fund-raising or educational use. For details, write Special Markets, Success Builders, Inc., P.O. Box 1686-101, Ellicott City, MD 21041.

ABOUT THE AUTHOR

Raymond L. Wenderlich did his undergraduate work at the U.S. Naval Academy; earned his master's degree in Engineering Administration from the George Washington University; and attended the Management Program for Executives at the University of Pittsburgh. He has enjoyed much success in a wide variety of leadership positions in such diverse disciplines as sales and service to large commercial, industrial, and government customers; commercial power plant operations, maintenance, and training; management systems; quality assurance; as well as naval nuclear propulsion. He holds a significant leadership position with the Baltimore Gas & Electric Company.

During his 24 years in leadership, his organizations have consistently succeeded. His teams have regularly turned in award-winning performances. His leadership style has been widely praised, especially by his principal customers — the people he has led. He has received a number of leadership awards recognizing his highly effective leadership style. He has taught leadership for the Baltimore Gas & Electric Company and for the U.S. Army.

He resides in Calvert County, Maryland, with his wife, Vicki, and their two children, Ray and Amy.

You may contact the author via

Success Builders, Inc.
P.O. Box 1686-101
Ellicott City, Maryland 21041